Table of Contents

2

Comprehension: Snow Is Cold!

Directions: Read about snow. Circle the answers.

When you play in snow, dress warmly. Wear a coat. Wear a hat. Wear gloves. Do you wear these when you play in snow?

1. Snow is   warm.
                                                 cold.

2. When you play in snow, dress   warmly.
                                                 quickly.

Directions: List three things to wear when you play in snow.

_____

- -

_____

- -

_____

- -

_____

Directions: Circle five things in picture #1 that are not in picture #2.

#1

#2

Sequencing: Make a Snowman!

Directions: Write the number of the sentence that goes with each picture in the box.

1. Roll a large snowball for the snowman's bottom.

2. Make another snowball and put it on top of the first.

3. Put the last snowball on top.

4. Dress the snowman.

Directions: Circle the two things that do not belong in the picture. Write why they do not belong.

1. _____

_____

_____

2. _____

_____

Classifying: These Keep Me Warm

Directions: Color the things that keep you warm.

socks

apple

lunch box

earmuffs

cookie

coat

umbrella

hat

gloves

book

Comprehension: Raking Leaves

Directions: Read about raking leaves. Then, answer the questions.

I like to rake leaves. Do you? Leaves die each year. They get brown and dry. They fall from the trees. Then, we rake them up.

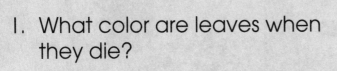

1. What color are leaves when they die?

   _____

   -

   _____

2. What happens when they die?

   _____

   -

   _____

   -

   _____

3. What do we do when leaves fall?

   _____

   -

   _____

Sequencing: Raking Leaves

Directions: Write a number in each box to show the order of the story.

Classifying: Leaves

Directions: Cut out the leaves. Put them into two groups. Glue each group in a box on the top of the page. Write a name for each group.

_____   _____

- - - - - - - - - - - - -   - - - - - - - - - - - - -

_____   _____

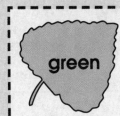
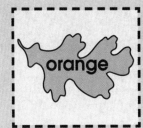

green

green

orange

green

orange

orange

orange

Directions: Read about flowers. Then, write the answers.

Some flowers grow in pots. Many flowers grow in flower beds. Others grow beside the road. Flowers begin from seeds. They grow into small buds. Then, they open wide and bloom. Flowers are pretty!

1. Name two places flowers grow.

_____

_____

_____

_____

2. Flowers begin from

_____

_____ .

3. Then, flowers grow into small

_____

_____ .

4. Flowers then open wide and

_____

_____ .

Flower Puzzle

Directions: Read the story about flowers again. Then, complete the puzzle.

Across:

2. Flowers do this when they open wide.
3. Flowers grow from these.

Down:

1. A flower can grow in a flower bed or a ___.
2. Before they bloom, flowers grow ___.

Sequencing: How Flowers Grow

Directions: Read the story. Then, write the steps to grow a flower.

First, find a sunny spot. Then, plant the seed. Water it. The flower will start to grow. Pull the weeds around it. Remember to keep giving the flower water. Enjoy your flower.

I. _____ .

2. _____ .

3. _____ .

4. _____ .

5. _____ .

Review

Directions: Write words in the blanks to make a label for a seed packet. Use ideas from the stories on pages 13 and 15 and your own ideas.

_____

_____ Seeds

Plant seeds in a

_____

_____ .

Give them lots of

_____

_____ .

A bud will grow. Then, it will

_____

_____ .

The flower will keep growing if you pull the

_____

_____ around it.

_____

Your flowers will be very _____ .

Directions: Read the story and look at the pictures. Then, write the answers.

Some clothes are for winter. Some clothes are for summer. Winter clothes keep us warm. Summer clothes keep us cool. In summer, I put on shorts, then a shirt, and then sandals. These clothes keep me cool!

shirt   coat   hat   sandals   shorts

                    scarf

1. Tell the order of clothes I put on in summer.

_____   _____   _____

- - - - - - - - - - -   - - - - - - - - - - -   - - - - - - - - - - -

_____   _____   _____

First   Then   Last

2. List the winter clothes pictured.

_____   _____   _____

- - - - - - - - - - -   - - - - - - - - - - -   - - - - - - - - - - -

_____   _____   _____

3. How are summer and winter clothes different?

Summer clothes   Winter clothes
keep us   keep us

_____   _____

- - - - - - - - - - - - -   - - - - - - - - - - - - -

_____ .   _____ .

Comprehension: Balloons

Directions: Read the story. Then, answer the questions.

Some balloons float. They are filled with gas. Some do not float. They are filled with air. Some clowns carry balloons. Balloons come in many colors. What color do you like?

1. What makes balloons float?

   _____

   -

   _____

2. What is in balloons that do not float?

   _____

   -

   _____

3. What shape are the balloons the clown is holding?

   _____

   -

   _____

Comprehension: Balloons

Directions: Read the story about balloons again. Draw a picture for the sentence in each box.

The clown is holding **red**, yellow, and **blue** balloons filled with air.

The clown is holding **purple**, orange, **green**, and **blue** balloons filled with gas.

Same and Different: Clowns

Directions: Look at the two clowns. Color the things in picture #2 that are different from the things in picture #1.

#1

#2

Directions: Color the clown.
Use your crayons this way:

    I — **red**

    2 — **blue**

    3 — **orange**

    4 — **pink**

Directions: Write the answers on the lines.

1. What color did you use for the clown's hair?

_____

- -

_____

2. What color is the clown's nose?

_____

- -

_____

3. What color is the clown's collar?

_____

- -

_____

4. What color is the clown's mouth?

_____

- -

_____

Classifying: Clowns and Balloons

Some words describe clowns. Some words describe balloons.

Directions: Read the words. Write the words that match in the correct columns.

float	laughs	hat	string
air	feet	pop	nose

clown

balloons

_____
_____
_____
_____
_____
_____
_____
_____
_____

_____
_____
_____
_____
_____
_____
_____
_____
_____

Directions: Read the story. Then, write the answers.

Do you like cats? I do. To pet a cat, move slowly. Hold out your hand. The cat will come to you. Then, pet its head. Do not grab a cat! It will run away.

To pet a cat . . .

_____

_____

1. Move _____ .

_____

2. Hold out your _____ .

_____

3. The cat will come to _____ .

_____

4. Pet the cat's _____ .

_____

5. Do not _____ a cat!

Comprehension: Cats

Directions: Read the story about cats again. Then, write the answers.

1. What is a good title for the story?

2. The story tells you how to

3. What part of your body should you pet a cat with?

4. Why should you move slowly to pet a cat?

5. Why do you think a cat will run away if you grab it?

Directions: Look at the pictures and read about four cats. Then, write the correct name beside each cat.

Fluffy, Blackie, and Tiger are playing. Tom is sleeping. Blackie has spots. Tiger has stripes.

Same and Different: Cats

Directions: Compare the picture of the cats on page 25 to this picture. Write a word from the box to tell what is different about each cat.

purple ball   green bow   blue brush   red collar

1. Tom is wearing a _____.

2. Blackie has a _____.

3. Fluffy is wearing a _____.

4. Tiger has a _____.

Directions: Read about tigers. Then, write the answers.

Tigers sleep during the day. They hunt at night. Tigers eat meat. They hunt deer. They like to eat wild pigs. If they cannot find meat, tigers will eat fish.

1. When do tigers sleep?

   _____

   -

   _____

2. Name two things tigers eat.

   _____

   -

   _____

   _____

   -

   _____

3. When do tigers hunt?

   _____

   -

   _____

Following Directions: Tiger Puzzle

Directions: Read the story about tigers again. Then, complete the puzzle.

Across:

1. When tigers cannot get meat, they eat ___.
3. The food tigers like best is ___.
4. Tigers like to eat this meat: wild ___.

Down:

2. Tigers do this during the day.

Directions: Follow directions to complete the picture of the tiger.

1. Draw **black** stripes on the tiger's body and tail.

2. Color the tiger's tongue **red**.

3. Draw claws on the feet.

4. Draw a **black** nose and two **black** eyes on the tiger's face.

5. Color the rest of the tiger orange.

6. Draw tall, green grass for the tiger to sleep in.

Directions: Read about skiing. Circle the answers. Write a number in each box to show the order of the story.

Skiing Is Fun

You need to dress warmly to ski. One ski fits on each boot. You wear the skis to a chair called a ski lift. It takes you up in the air to a hill. When you get off, you ski down the hill. Be careful! Sometimes you will fall.

1. To ski, you need

   two skis.
   one ski.

2. Skiing is an

   indoor sport.
   outdoor sport.

Directions: Read about apples. Then, write the answers.

I like . Do you?   Some  are red.

Some  are green.   Some are yellow.

1. How many kinds of apples does the story tell about?

   _____

   -

   _____

2. Name the kinds of apples.

   _____   _____

   - - - - - - - - - - - - - - - -   - - - - - - - - - - - - - - - -

   _____   _____

   - - - - - - - - - - - - - - - -

   _____

3. What kind of apple do you like best?

   _____

   -

   _____

Classifying: Fruit

Fruit tastes good. It is sweet. Fruit is a good snack.

Directions: Look at the words and pictures. Then, write the names of the fruits in the blanks.

apple

banana

grapes

potato

orange

carrot

broccoli

Classifying: Vegetables

Vegetables grow in gardens. Vegetables help keep us healthy.

Directions: Look at the pictures. Then, write the name of the vegetables in the blanks.

beans

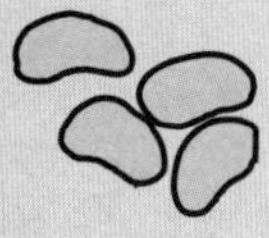

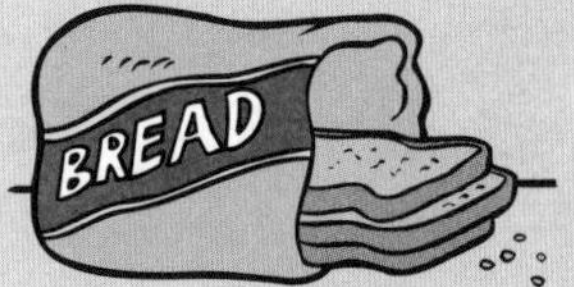

bread

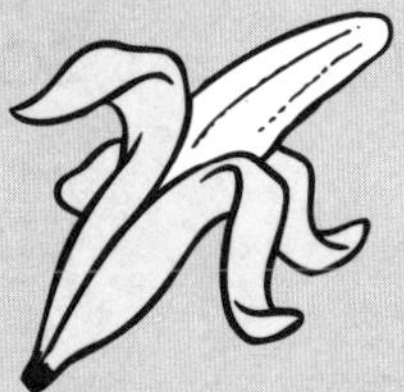

banana

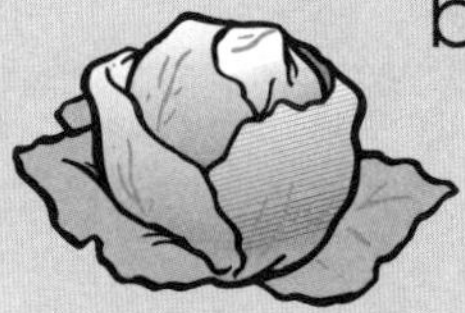

lettuce

carrot

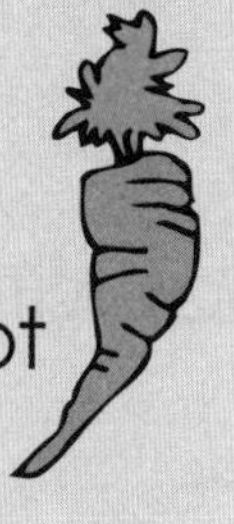

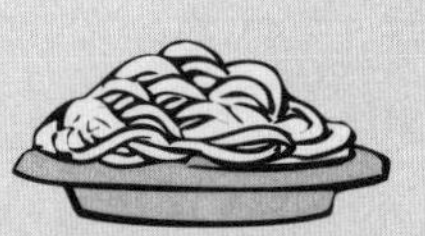

noodles

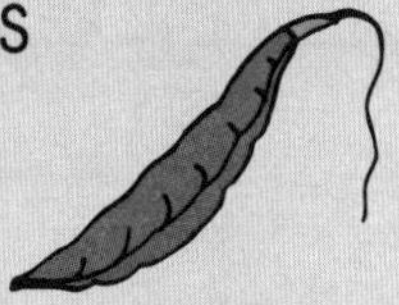

peas

broccoli

Add the name of one more vegetable.

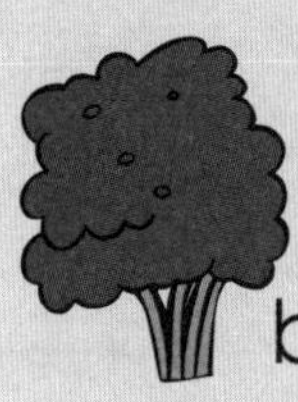

Directions: Read the story. Use words from the box to answer the questions.

People eat with spoons and forks. They use a spoon to eat soup and ice cream. They use a fork to eat potatoes. They use a knife to cut their meat. They say, "Thank you. It was good!" when they finish.

| fork | ice cream | knife | soup |

1. What do we use to cut food?

   _____

   _____

   _____

2. What are two things you can eat with a spoon?

   _____ _____

   _____ _____

   _____ _____

3. What do we use to eat meat and potatoes?

   _____

   _____

   _____

Directions: Read the questions under each plate. Draw three foods on each plate to answer the questions.

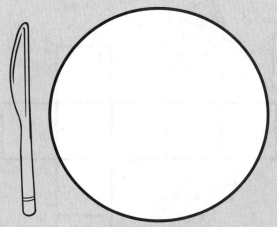

1. What foods can you cut with a knife?

2. What foods should you eat with a fork?

3. What foods can you eat with a spoon?

Directions: Write each word next to its picture in the puzzle.

1. bag
2. apple
3. bird
4. cookie

Directions: Complete the sentences. Write the answers in the blanks.

5. I can carry things in a _____ .

6. I like to eat a red _____ .

7. I wish I could fly like a _____ .

8. I can bake a _____ .

Directions: Circle the pictures in each row that belong together.

Row 1   knife   key   fork   spoon

Row 2   orange   apple   candy   banana

Directions: Write the names of the pictures that do not belong.

Row 1 _____

Row 2 _____

Classifying: Why They Are Different

Directions: Look at your answers on page 37. Write why each object does not belong.

_____

- -

Row 1 _____

_____

- -

Row 2 _____

Directions: For each object, draw a group of pictures that belong with it.

candy bar

lettuce

Directions: Read about the party. Then, complete the invitation.

The party will be at Dog's house. The party will start at 1:00 p.m. It will last two hours. Write your birthday for the date of the party.

Party Invitation

_____

- -

Where: _____

_____

- -

Date: _____

_____

- -

Time It Begins: _____

_____

- -

Time It Ends: _____

Sequencing: Pig Gets Ready

Directions: Number the pictures of Pig getting ready for the party to show the order of the story.

What kind of party do you think Pig is going to?

_____

_____

Directions: Use the picture for clues. Write words from the box to answer the questions.

bear
dog
giraffe
pig
cat
elephant
hippo
tiger

1. Which animals have bow ties?

_____   _____

-     -

_____   _____

2. Which animal has a hat?

_____

- -

_____

3. Which animal has a striped shirt?

_____

- -

_____

Classifying: Party Items

Directions: Draw a ☐ around objects that are food for the party. Draw a △ around the party guests. Draw a ○ around the objects used for fun at the party.

ice cream   candy   games   tiger

noise makers   cake   garbage can   cat

glasses   candle   bear   juice

balloons   giraffe   hat   pig

potato chips   hippo

Directions: Read about cookies. Then, write your answers.

Cookies are made with many things. All cookies are made with flour. Some cookies have nuts in them. Some cookies do not. Some cookies have chocolate chips. Some do not. Cookbooks give directions on how to make cookies.

First, turn on the oven. Then, get out all the things that go in the cookies. Mix them together. Roll them out, and cut the cookies. Bake the cookies. Now, eat them!

1. Tell one way all cookies are the same.

   _____

   -

   _____

2. Name one different thing in cookies.

   _____

   -

   _____

3. Where do you find directions for making cookies?

   _____

   -

   _____

Comprehension: The Teddy Bear Song

Do you know the Teddy Bear Song? It is very old!

Directions: Read the Teddy Bear Song. Then, answer the questions.

Teddy bear, teddy bear, turn around.

Teddy bear, teddy bear, touch the ground.

Teddy bear, teddy bear, climb upstairs.

Teddy bear, teddy bear, say your prayers.

Teddy bear, teddy bear, turn out the light.

Teddy bear, teddy bear, say, "Good night!"

1. What is the first thing the teddy bear does?

    _____

    _____

2. What is the last thing the teddy bear does?

    _____

    _____

3. What would you name a teddy bear?

    _____

    _____

Directions: Color and cut out the teddy bear. Act out the song on page 44 with your teddy bear.

Directions: Write words to make a new teddy bear song. Act out your new song with your teddy bear as you read it.

Teddy bear, teddy bear, turn

_____

- -

_____ .

Teddy bear, teddy bear, touch the

_____

- -

_____ .

Teddy bear, teddy bear, climb

_____

- -

_____ .

Teddy bear, teddy bear, turn out

_____

- -

_____ .

Teddy bear, teddy bear, say,

_____

- -

_____ .

Sequencing: Put Teddy Bear to Bed

Directions: Read the song about the teddy bear again. Write a number in each box to show the order of the story.

Directions: Read how to play Simon Says. Then, answer the questions.

Simon Says

Here is how to play Simon Says: One kid is Simon. Simon is the leader. Everyone must do what Simon says and does, but only if the leader says, "Simon says" first. Let's try it. "Simon says, 'Pat your head.'" "Simon says, 'Pat your nose. Pat your toes.'" Oops! Did you pat your toes? I did not say, "Simon says," first. If you patted your toes, you are out!

1. Who is the leader in this game?

   _____

   _____

2. What must the leader say first each time?

   _____

   _____

3. What happens if you do something and the leader did not say, "Simon says"?

   _____

   _____

Directions: Read each sentence. Look at the picture next to it. Circle the picture if the person is playing Simon Says correctly.

1. Simon says, "Put your hands on your hips."

2. Simon says, "Stand on one leg."

3. Simon says, "Put your hands on your head."

4. Simon says, "Ride a bike."

5. Simon says, "Jump up and down."

6. Simon says, "Pet a dog."

Directions: Read the sentences. If Simon tells you to do something, follow the directions. If Simon does not tell you to do something, go to the next sentence.

1. Simon says: Cross out all the numbers 2 through 9.

2. Simon says: Cross out the vowel that is in the word "sun."

3. Cross out the letter "B."

4. Cross out the vowels "A" and "E."

5. Simon says: Cross out the consonants in the word "cup."

6. Cross out the letter "Z."

7. Simon says: Cross out all the "K's."

8. Simon says: Read your message.

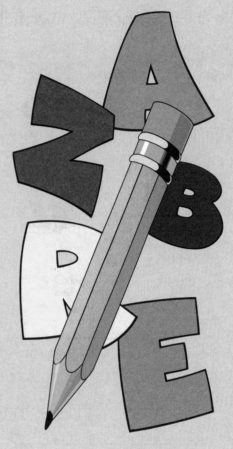

C 3 G U 7 P R U C P E K C P A 8 K K

6 T P U P J C 5 P O K 9 P B U P K K

Same and Different: Look at Simon

Directions: Find four things in picture #2 that are not in picture #1. Write your answers. Use words from the box.

hat	head	bare feet	socks
feather	watch	untied shoes	shirt

#1

#2

1. _____

2. _____

3. _____

4. _____

Directions: Read about crayons. Then, write your answers.

Crayons come in many colors. Some crayons are dark colors. Some crayons are light colors. All crayons have wax in them.

1. How many colors of crayons are there?

   many

   few

   _____

   -

2. Crayons come in _____

   _____

   -

   colors and _____colors.

3. What do all crayons have in them?

   _____

   -

   _____

Following Directions: Hidden Picture

Directions: To find the hidden picture, color only the shapes with a number inside.

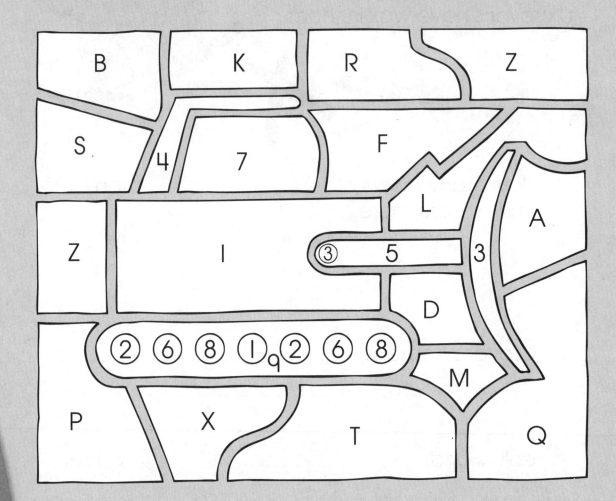

Directions: Read about words that rhyme. Then, circle the answers.

Words that rhyme have the same end sounds. "Wing" and "sing" rhyme. "Boy" and "toy" rhyme. "Dime" and "time" rhyme. Can you think of other words that rhyme?

TREE, SEE
SHOE, BLUE
KITE, BITE
MAKE, TAKE
FLY, BUY

1. Words that rhyme have the same   end sounds.

          end letters.

2. "Time" rhymes with   "tree."

          "dime."

Directions: Write one rhyme for each word.

wing
_____

boy
_____

dime
_____

pink
_____

Classifying: Rhymes

Directions: Circle the pictures in each row that rhyme.

Row 1

Row 2

Row 3

Directions: Write the names of the pictures that do not rhyme.

These words do not rhyme:

Row 1   Row 2   Row 3

_____   _____   _____

-------------------   -------------------   -------------------

_____   _____   _____

Directions: Cut out the pieces. Read the words. Find two words that rhyme. Put the words together.

kite

my

tree

bell

buy

bee

well

white

Directions: Read about ways you move. Circle the correct answer.

You can move in many ways. You can run. When you run, one foot hits the ground at a time. You can jump. When you jump, you land on two feet. You can hop. To hop, first stand on one leg. Then, jump up and down.

1. Running and jumping are different because:

One foot hits the ground at a time when you run. Two feet hit the ground at a time when you jump.

Two feet hit the ground at a time when you run. One foot hits the ground at a time when you jump.

Directions: Write directions on how to hop.

_____

_____

2. First, _____ .

_____

3. Then, _____ .

Directions: Read about babies. Then, write the answers.

Babies are small. Some babies cry a lot. They cry when they are wet. They cry when they are hungry. They smile when they are dry. They smile when they are fed.

1. Name two reasons babies cry.

   _____   _____

   - - - - - - - - - - - - - -   - - - - - - - - - - - - - -

   _____   _____

2. Name two reasons babies smile.

   _____   _____

   - - - - - - - - - - - - - -   - - - - - - - - - - - - - -

   _____   _____

3. Write a baby's name you like.

   _____

   -

   _____

Directions: Read each sentence. Draw a picture of a baby's face in the box to show if she would cry or smile.

1. The baby needs to have her diaper changed.

2. The baby has not eaten for awhile.

3. Dad put a dry diaper on the baby.

4. The baby is going to finish her bottle.

5. The baby finished her food but is still hungry.

Sequencing: Feeding Baby

Directions: Read the sentences. Write a number in each box to show the order of the story.

The baby smiles.

Mom makes the baby's food.

The baby is put in his chair.

The baby is crying.

Mom feeds the baby.

Directions: Read the story. Then, use the words in the box and the picture to write your answers.

Ben and Ann are twin babies. They were born at the same time. They have the same mother. Ben is a boy baby. Ann is a girl baby.

mother   bow   boy   girl   hat   twins

1. Ann and Ben have the same

_____

_____ .

_____

------------------------- .

2. Ann and Ben are _____ .

3. Ann is a   Ben is a

_____   _____

---------------   ---------------

_____ .   _____ .

4. Ann is wearing a   Ben is wearing a

_____   _____

---------------   ---------------

_____ .   _____ .

Comprehension: Hats

Directions: Read about hats. Then, write your answers.

There are many kinds of hats. Some baseball hats have brims. Some fancy hats have feathers. Some knit hats pull down over your ears. Some hats are made of straw. Do you like hats?

1. Name four kinds of hats.

_____   _____

- - - - - - - - - - - - - - - - -   - - - - - - - - - - - - - - - - -

_____   _____

- - - - - - - - - - - - - - - - -   - - - - - - - - - - - - - - - - -

_____   _____

Directions: Circle the correct answers.

2. What kind of hats pull down over your ears?

   straw hats

   knit hats

3. What are some hats made of?

   straw

   mud

Sequencing: Choosing a Hat

Directions: Write a number in each box to show the order of the story.

Classifying: Hats

Directions: A store has four types of hats. Draw three hats for each type listed. Write what kind of hats you think should be in the last group, and draw three of that kind.

Tall Hats

Hats With Points

Fancy Hats

Classifying: Mr. Lincoln's Hat

Abraham Lincoln wore a tall hat. He liked to keep things in his hat so he would not lose them.

Directions: Cut out the pictures of things Mr. Lincoln could have kept in his hat. Glue those pictures on the hat.

letters	candle	penny	one dollar
bowl	cat	watch	paper

Directions: Draw a hat on each person. Read the sentences to know what kind of hat to draw.

1. The first girl is wearing a purple hat with feathers.

2. The boy next to the girl with the purple hat is wearing a red baseball hat.

3. The first boy is wearing a yellow knit hat.

4. The last boy is wearing a brown top hat.

5. The girl next to the boy with the red hat is wearing a blue straw hat.

Review

Directions: Read the story. Then, circle the pictures of things that are wet.

Some things used in baking are dry. Some things used in baking are wet. To bake a cake, first mix the salt, sugar, and flour. Then, add the egg. Now, add the milk. Stir. Put the cake in the oven.

Directions: Tell the order to mix things when you bake a cake.

1. _____   4. _____

2. _____   5. _____

3. _____

Directions: Circle the answers.

6. The first things to mix are   dry.   wet.

7. Where are cakes baked?   oven   grill

Directions: Read the story. Then, complete the puzzle.

The Zoo and the Farm

The zoo is for wild animals. Tigers live at the zoo. Some snakes live at the zoo. The farm is for tame animals. Ducks and donkeys live on farms.

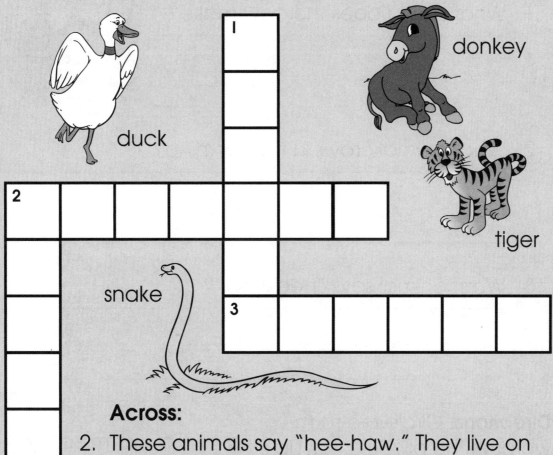

duck

donkey

tiger

snake

Across:

2. These animals say "hee-haw." They live on the farm.
3. These animals are long and thin. Some live in the zoo.

Down:

1. These animal have stripes. They live in the zoo.
2. These animals say "quack." They live on the farm.

Comprehension: Farm Sounds

Directions: Read the story. Then, answer the questions.

You can hear many sounds on the farm. Roosters crow in the morning. The cows moo, and donkeys say, "hee-haw." You might even hear the tractor motor humming.

1. What sound does the cow make?

2. What animal crows in the morning?

3. What animal says "hee-haw"?

Directions: Circle the farm words in the puzzle. Look up and down and sideways.

donkey	rooster
moo	tractor

```
a  l  b  x  m  d  y
e  u  m  p  o  o  a
k  c  f  h  o  n  j
q  k  t  u  l  k  w
r  o  o  s  t  e  r
c  e  n  o  s  y  v
t  r  a  c  t  o  r
```

Directions: Look at the pictures of the barnyards. Color the five things in picture #1 that are different from picture #2.

#1

#2

Comprehension: Animals

Directions: Read about inside and outside animals. Circle the pictures of animals that can live inside.

Some animals belong inside. Some animals belong outside. Wild animals belong outside. Large animals belong outside. Small, tame animals can live inside.

Directions: Write the names of animals that belong outside.

tiger

parakeets

ostrich

cat

cow

horse

1. _____

2. _____

3. _____

4. _____

Directions: Read about the days of the week. Then, answer the questions.

Do you know the names of the seven days of the week? Here they are: Sunday, Monday, Tuesday, Wednesday, Thursday, Friday, and Saturday.

1. What day comes after Thursday?

   _____

   _____

2. What day comes before Tuesday?

   _____

   _____

3. How many days are in each week?

   _____

   _____

Calendars show the days of the week in order. Sunday comes first. Saturday comes last. There are five days in between. An **abbreviation** is a short way of writing words. The abbreviations for the days of the week are usually the first three or four letters of the word followed by a period.

Example: Sunday — Sun.

Directions: Write the days of the week in order on the calendar. Use the abbreviations.

Day 1	Day 2	Day 3
Sunday	Monday	Tuesday
Sun.		Tues.

Day 4	Day 5	Day 6
Wednesday	Thursday	Friday
	Thurs.	

Day 7
Saturday

Directions: Read about boats. Then, answer the questions.

See the boats! They float on water. Some boats have sails. The wind moves the sails. It makes the boats go. Many people name their sailboats. They paint the name on the side of the boat.

1. What makes sailboats move?

_____

- -

_____

2. Where do sailboats float?

_____

- -

_____

3. What would you name a sailboat?

_____

- -

_____

Same and Different: Color the Boats

Directions: Find the three boats that are alike. Color them all the same. One boat is different. Color it differently.

Comprehension: A Boat Ride

Directions: Write a sentence under each picture to tell what is happening. Read the story you wrote.

Directions: Read the story. Then, answer the questions.

Let's Take a Trip!

Pack your bag. Shall we go by car, plane, or train? Let's go to the sea. When we get there, let's go on a sailboat.

1. What are three ways to travel?

   _____   _____

   _____   _____

   _____   _____

   _____

2. Where will we go?

   _____

   _____

3. What will we do when we get there?

   _____

   _____

Directions: Read about how to get to the beach. Use a crayon to draw the path to the beach.

Let's Go to the Beach

On the way to the beach, you will stop for food, then gas. Next, you cross a bridge. Finally, you will be at the beach!

Review

Directions: Read the story. Then, write the answers.

Fun With Balls

Some balls are soft. A beach ball is soft. Some balls are hard. We play baseball with a hard ball. Basketballs bounce. Can you throw a basketball through a hoop? First, bounce it three times. Then, hold the basketball high. Now, throw it toward the hoop. Did you make a basket?

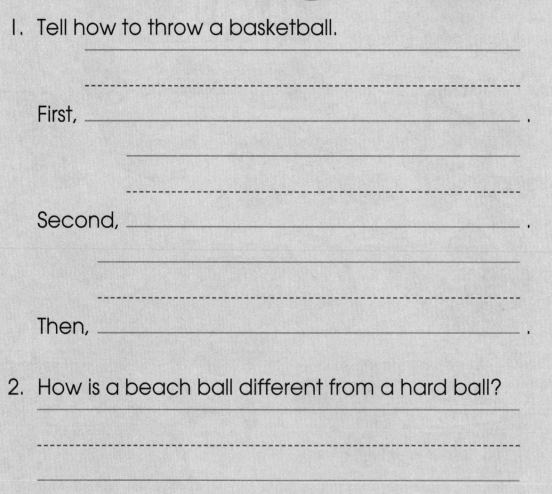

1. Tell how to throw a basketball.

_____

_____

First, _____ .

_____

Second, _____ .

_____

Then, _____ .

2. How is a beach ball different from a hard ball?

_____

_____

Directions: Read about clocks. Then, answer the questions.

Ticking Clocks

Many clocks make two sounds. The sounds are tick and tock. Big clocks often make loud tick-tocks. Little clocks often make quiet tick-tocks. Sometimes people put little clocks in a box with a new puppy. The puppy likes the sound. The tick-tock makes the puppy feel safe.

1. What two sounds do many clocks make?

_____   _____

-------------------------   -------------------------

_____ and _____

2. What kind of tick-tocks do big clocks make?

_____

- -

_____

3. What kind of clock makes a new puppy feel safe?

_____

- -

_____

Sequencing: Help the Puppy Feel Safe

Directions: Read the story about clocks again. Then, write a number in each box to show the order of the story.

Directions: Circle the pictures in each row that go together.

Row 1   cookies   cake   beans   ice cream

Row 2   apple   banana   orange   cookies

Directions: Write the names of the things that do not belong.

Row 1 _____

Row 2 _____

Classifying: Things to Drink

Directions: Circle the pictures of things you can drink. Write the names of those things in the blanks.

milk

ice

soup and crackers

juice

soda

ice-cream bar

Directions: Draw a line from the pictures of things you chew to the plate.

soup

ice-cream bar

pizza

carrot

soda

macaroni

gum

corn on the cob

milk

Comprehension: Soup

Directions: Read about soup. Then, write the answers.

I Like Soup

Soup is good! It is good for you, too. We eat most kinds of soup hot. Some people eat cold soup in the summer. Carrots and beans are in some soups. Do you like crackers with soup?

1. Name two ways people eat soup.

   _____ _____

   _____ _____

2. Name two things that are in some soups.

   _____ _____

   _____ _____

3. Name the kind of soup you like best.

   _____

   _____

Same and Different: Soup

Directions: Circle the five things in picture #1 that are not in picture #2.

#1

#2

Comprehension: The Three Bears

Directions: Read about the three bears. Put #1 beside Papa Bear's bed. Put #2 beside Mama Bear's bed. Put #3 beside Baby Bear's bed.

The Three Bears

Do you know the story of the three bears? Papa Bear is the biggest bear. He has the biggest bed. Mama Bear is a middle-size bear. She has a middle-size bed. Baby Bear is the little bear. He has the smallest bed.

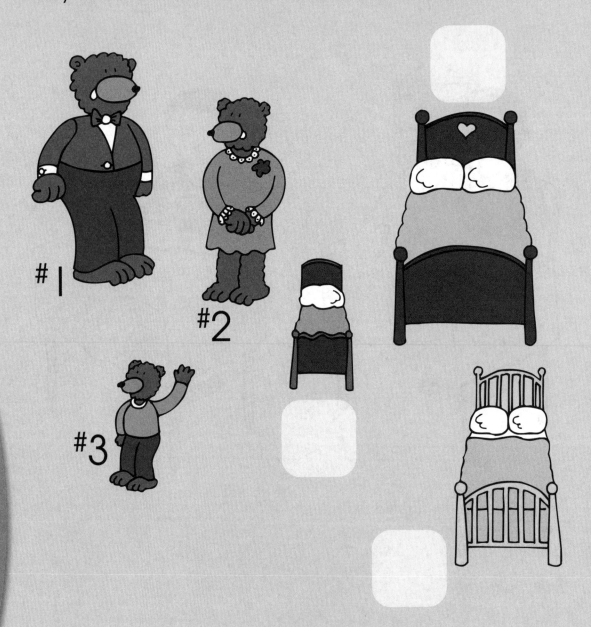

#1

#2

#3

Comprehension: The Three Bears

Directions: Draw the objects that belong to the three bears. Then, complete the sentences.

Draw the bowls.

Baby	Mama	Papa

Mama's bowl is _____ than Papa's.

Mama's bowl is _____ than Baby's.

Draw the chairs.

Papa	Mama	Baby

Papa's chair is _____ than Baby's.

Baby's chair is _____ than Mama's.

Following Directions: Three Bears Puzzle

Directions: Read the story about the three bears again. Then, complete the puzzle.

Across:

1. Papa Bear is the ___ bear.
3. All the bears sleep in ___.

Down:

1. This bear is the little bear.
2. Mama Bear is the middle-___ bear.

Directions: Read how to make no-cook candy. Then, answer the questions.

Some candy needs to be cooked on a stove. You do not need to cook this kind of candy. It is easy to make. You will need a large bowl for mixing. You will need five things to make this candy.

No-Cook Candy

$\frac{1}{2}$ cup peanut butter

4 cups powdered sugar

1 cup cocoa

pinch of salt

4 tablespoons milk

Mix everything in the bowl. Roll it into small balls. (A pinch of salt is just a tiny bit.)

1. What is third on the list of things needed?

   _____

   -

   _____

2. What is different about no-cook candy?

   _____

   -

   _____

Directions: Write what to do to make no-cook candy.

3. First, mix everything in a bowl. Then,

   _____

   -

   _____

Comprehension: "Humpty Dumpty"

Directions: Read the poem. Draw a picture of Humpty Dumpty after he fell off the wall.

Humpty Dumpty sat on a wall.

Humpty Dumpty had a great fall.

All the king's horses and all the king's men

Couldn't put Humpty together again.

Directions: Cut out the pieces and mix them up. Then, read the sentence on each piece to put Humpty back together.

Humpty was sitting on a wall.

Humpty fell off the wall.

The king's horses and men tried to put Humpty together.

Humpty couldn't be put together.

Directions: Read "Hey Diddle Diddle." Then, answer the questions.

Hey diddle diddle,

The cat and the fiddle,

The cow jumped over the moon.

The little dog laughed

To see such sport,

And the dish ran away with the spoon!

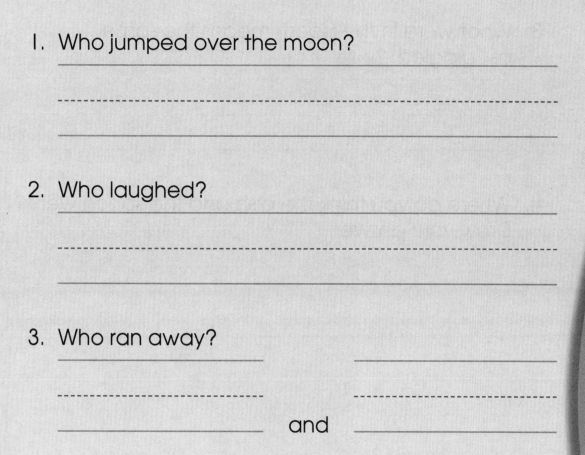

1. Who jumped over the moon?

_____

- -

_____

2. Who laughed?

_____

- -

_____

3. Who ran away?

_____   _____

- - - - - - - - - - - - - - - - -   - - - - - - - - - - - - -

_____ and _____

Comprehension: "Hey Diddle Diddle"

Directions: Read "Hey Diddle Diddle" again. Then, answer the questions.

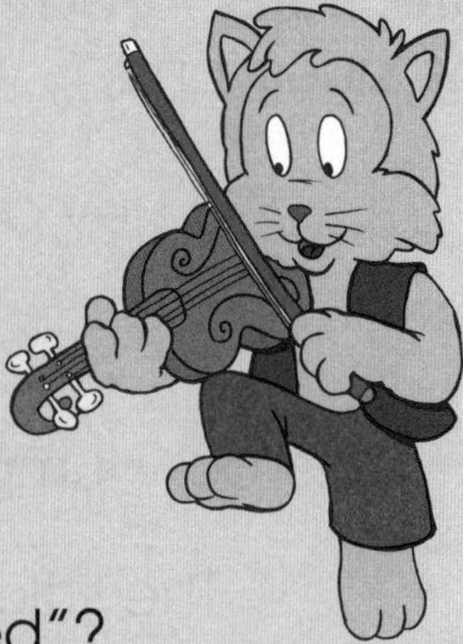

1. What is a fiddle?

2. What is another word for "jumped"?

3. What word in the poem means the same as "giggled"?

4. Where do you think the dish and the spoon went? Draw your answer.

Directions: Number the pictures for "Hey Diddle Diddle" in order.

Comprehension: "Bluebird"

Directions: Read the bluebird poem. Look at the picture. Write what the bluebird sees. Use words from the box.

Bluebird, bluebird,

Up in the tree,

How many blue things

Do you see?

book	flowers
girl	grass
hat	sky
shoes	tree

Here are the blue things the bluebird sees:

1. _____

2. _____

3. _____

4. _____

5. _____

Directions: Fill in the blanks to create a poem about a different colored bird. Then, draw a picture in the box to go with your poem.

_____   _____

_____ bird, _____ bird,

_____

Up in the _____ ,

_____

How many _____ things

Do you see?

Directions: Fill in the blanks.

_____

How many _____ things did the bird

_____

see in your picture? _____

Sequencing: Make an Ice-Cream Cone

Directions: Number the boxes in order to show how to make an ice-cream cone.

Comprehension: Eating Ice Cream

Directions: Read the story. Write two things Sam could have done so he could have enjoyed eating his ice-cream cone.

It was a hot day. Sam went to the store and got an ice-cream cone. He ate it at a table in the sun. Sam watched some friends play ball. When he went to eat his ice-cream, it had melted and fallen on the sidewalk.

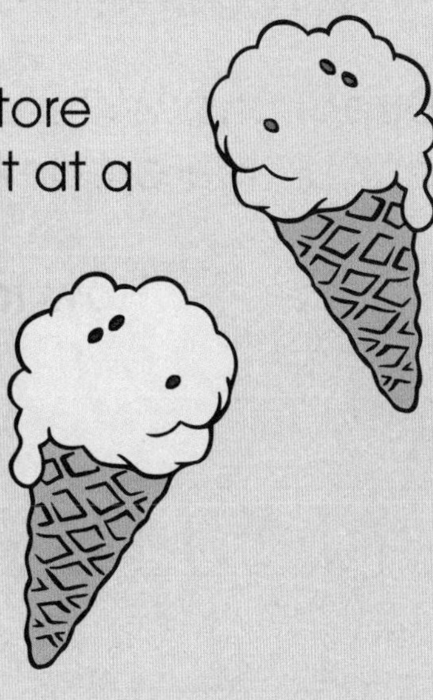

1.

2.

Sequencing: Eating a Cone

What if a person never ate an ice-cream cone? Could you tell them how to eat it? Think about what you do when you eat an ice-cream cone.

Directions: Write directions to teach someone how to eat an ice-cream cone.

How to Eat an Ice-Cream Cone

1. _____

2. _____

3. _____

4. _____

Directions: Read about coins. Then, answer the questions.

You can use coins to buy things. Some coins are worth more than others. Do you know these coins? A penny is worth one cent. A nickel is worth five cents. A dime is worth 10 cents. A quarter is worth 25 cents.

1. What can you use coins to do?

_____

_____

2. How are coins different?

_____

_____

Directions: Number the coins in order from the one that is worth the least to the one that is worth the most. Under each picture, write how many cents each coin is worth.

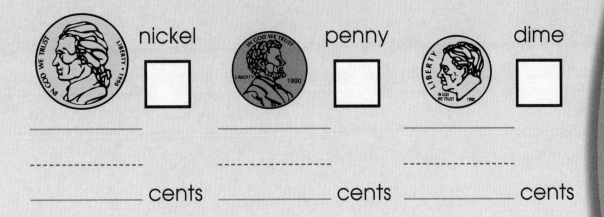

nickel ☐   penny ☐   dime ☐

_____ cents   _____ cents   _____ cents

Glossary

Abbreviation: A short way of writing words. Examples: **Mon., Tues.,** etc.

Classifying: Putting objects, words, or ideas that are alike into categories.

Comprehension: Understanding what is seen, heard, or read.

Following Directions: Doing what the directions say to do.

Same and Different: Being able to tell how things are alike and not alike.

Sequencing: Putting things in order.

4 — Comprehension: Snow Is Cold!

Directions: Read about snow. Circle the answers.

When you play in snow, dress warmly. Wear a coat. Wear a hat. Wear gloves. Do you wear these when you play in snow?

1. Snow is
   warm.
   cold.

2. When you play in snow, dress
   warmly.
   quickly.

Directions: List three things to wear when you play in snow.

Answers may include:

hat, scarf, coat, gloves or mittens, boots, snowpants

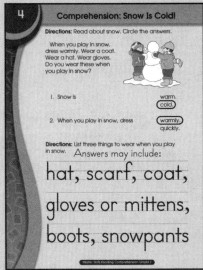

4

5 — Same and Different

Directions: Circle five things in picture #1 that are not in picture #2.

5

6 — Sequencing: Make a Snowman!

Directions: Write the number of the sentence that goes with each picture in the box.

1. Roll a large snowball for the snowman's bottom.
2. Make another snowball and put it on top of the first.
3. Put the last snowball on top.
4. Dress the snowman.

6

7 — Classifying: What Does Not Belong?

Directions: Circle the two things that do not belong in the picture. Write why they do not belong.

1. Flowers do not grow in snow.
2. Palm trees do not grow in snow.

7

8 — Classifying: These Keep Me Warm

Directions: Color the things that keep you warm.

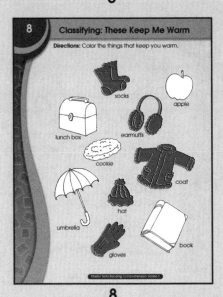

socks
apple
lunch box
earmuffs
cookie
coat
umbrella
hat
gloves
book

8

9 — Comprehension: Raking Leaves

Directions: Read about raking leaves. Then, answer the questions.

I like to rake leaves. Do you? Leaves die each year. They get brown and dry. They fall from the trees. Then, we rake them up.

1. What color are leaves when they die?

brown

2. What happens when they die?

They get dry and fall from the tree.

3. What do we do when leaves fall?

We rake them.

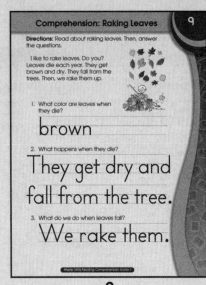

9

10 — Sequencing: Raking Leaves

Directions: Write a number in each box to show the order of the story.

10

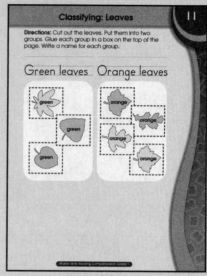

11 — Classifying: Leaves

Directions: Cut out the leaves. Put them into two groups. Glue each group in a box on the top of the page. Write a name for each group.

Green leaves   Orange leaves

11

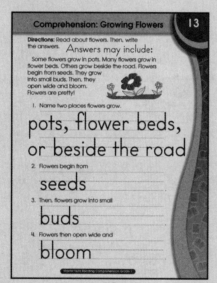

13 — Comprehension: Growing Flowers

Directions: Read about flowers. Then, write the answers. Answers may include:

Some flowers grow in pots. Many flowers grow in flower beds. Others grow beside the road. Flowers begin from seeds. They grow into small buds. Then, they open wide and bloom. Flowers are pretty!

1. Name two places flowers grow.

pots, flower beds, or beside the road

2. Flowers begin from

seeds

3. Then, flowers grow into small

buds

4. Flowers then open wide and

bloom

13

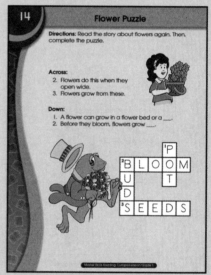

14 — Flower Puzzle

Directions: Read the story about flowers again. Then, complete the puzzle.

Across:
2. Flowers do this when they open wide.
3. Flowers grow from these.

Down:
1. A flower can grow in a flower bed or a ___.
2. Before they bloom, flowers grow ___.

Across 2. BLOOM 3. SEEDS
Down 1. POT 2. BUD

14

15 — Sequencing: How Flowers Grow

Directions: Read the story. Then, write the steps to grow a flower.

First, find a sunny spot. Then, plant the seed. Water it. The flower will start to grow. Pull the weeds around it. Remember to keep giving the flower water. Enjoy your flower.

Find a sunny spot
Plant the seed
Water it
Pull the weeds
Enjoy your flowers

15

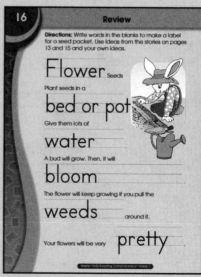

16 — Review

Directions: Write words in the blanks to make a label for a seed packet. Use ideas from the stories on pages 13 and 15 and your own ideas.

Flower Seeds

Plant seeds in a

bed or pot

Give them lots of

water

A bud will grow. Then, it will

bloom

The flower will keep growing if you pull the

weeds around it.

Your flowers will be very pretty

16

17 — Review

Directions: Read the story and look at the pictures. Then, write the answers.

Some clothes are for winter. Some clothes are for summer. Winter clothes keep us warm. Summer clothes keep us cool. In summer, I put on shorts, then a shirt, and then sandals. These clothes keep me cool!

shirt   coat   hat   sandals   shorts   scarf

1. Tell the order of clothes I put on in summer.

shorts shirt sandals
First   Then   Last

2. List the winter clothes pictured.

scarf coat hat

3. How are summer and winter clothes different?

Summer clothes keep us   **cool**

Winter clothes keep us   **warm**

Master Skills Reading Comprehension Grade 1

17

18 — Comprehension: Balloons

Directions: Read the story. Then, answer the questions.

Some balloons float. They are filled with gas. Some do not float. They are filled with air. Some clowns carry balloons. Balloons come in many colors. What color do you like?

1. What makes balloons float?

gas

2. What is in balloons that do not float?

air

3. What shape are the balloons the clown is holding?

circle

Master Skills Reading Comprehension Grade 1

18

19 — Comprehension: Balloons

Directions: Read the story about balloons again. Draw a picture for the sentence in each box.

The clown is holding red, yellow, and blue balloons filled with air.

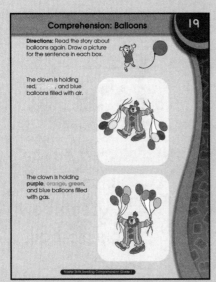

The clown is holding **purple**, orange, green, and blue balloons filled with gas.

Master Skills Reading Comprehension Grade 1

19

20 — Same and Different: Clowns

Directions: Look at the two clowns. Color the things in picture #2 that are different from the things in picture #1.

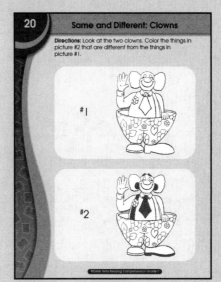

#1

#2

Master Skills Reading Comprehension Grade 1

20

21 — Following Directions: Color the Clown

Directions: Color the clown. Use your crayons this way:

1 — red
2 — blue
3 — orange
4 — pink

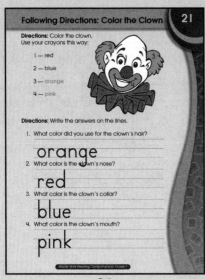

Directions: Write the answers on the lines.

1. What color did you use for the clown's hair?

orange

2. What color is the clown's nose?

red

3. What color is the clown's collar?

blue

4. What color is the clown's mouth?

pink

Master Skills Reading Comprehension Grade 1

21

22 — Classifying: Clowns and Balloons

Some words describe clowns. Some words describe balloons.

Directions: Read the words. Write the words that match in the correct columns.

| float | laughs | hat | string |
| air | feet | pop | nose |

clown	balloons
laughs	float
feet	air
hat	pop
nose	string

Master Skills Reading Comprehension Grade 1

22

Sequencing: Petting a Cat — 23

Directions: Read the story. Then, write the answers.

Do you like cats? I do. To pet a cat, move slowly. Hold out your hand. The cat will come to you. Then, pet its head. Do not grab a cat! It will run away.

To pet a cat . . .

1. Move **slowly**
2. Hold out your **hand**
3. The cat will come to **you**.
4. Pet the cat's **head**
5. Do not **grab** a cat!

Master Skills Reading Comprehension Grade 1

23

Comprehension: Cats — 24

Directions: Read the story about cats again. Then, write the answers.

1. What is a good title for the story?

Answers will vary.

2. The story tells you how to

pet a cat

3. What part of your body should you pet a cat with?

your hand

4. Why should you move slowly to pet a cat?

Answers will vary.

5. Why do you think a cat will run away if you grab it?

Answers will vary.

Master Skills Reading Comprehension Grade 1

24

Comprehension: Cats — 25

Directions: Look at the pictures and read about four cats. Then, write the correct name beside each cat.

Fluffy, Blackie, and Tiger are playing. Tom is sleeping. Blackie has spots. Tiger has stripes.

Fluffy

Tiger

Blackie

Tom

Master Skills Reading Comprehension Grade 1

25

Same and Different: Cats — 26

Directions: Compare the picture of the cats on page 25 to this picture. Write a word from the box to tell what is different about each cat.

| purple ball | green bow | blue brush | red collar |

1. Tom is wearing a **red collar**
2. Blackie has **blue brush**
3. Fluffy is wearing a **green bow**
4. Tiger has a **purple ball**

Master Skills Reading Comprehension Grade 1

26

Comprehension: Tigers — 27

Directions: Read about tigers. Then, write the answers.

Tigers sleep during the day. They hunt at night. Tigers eat meat. They hunt deer. They like to eat wild pigs. If they cannot find meat, tigers will eat fish.

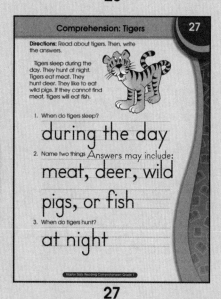

1. When do tigers sleep?

during the day

2. Name two things **Answers may include:** **meat, deer, wild pigs, or fish**

3. When do tigers hunt?

at night

Master Skills Reading Comprehension Grade 1

27

Following Directions: Tiger Puzzle — 28

Directions: Read the story about tigers again. Then, complete the puzzle.

Crossword puzzle:
- ¹FISH
- ²SLEEP
- MEAT
- ³PIG

Across:
1. When tigers cannot get meat, they eat ___.
3. The food tigers like best is ___.
4. Tigers like to eat this meat: wild ___.

Down:
2. Tigers do this during the day.

Master Skills Reading Comprehension Grade 1

28

Master Skills Reading Comprehension Grade 1

Answer Key

Following Directions: Draw a Tiger 29

Directions: Follow directions to complete the picture of the tiger.

1. Draw black stripes on the tiger's body and tail.
2. Color the tiger's tongue red.
3. Draw claws on the feet.
4. Draw a black nose and two black eyes on the tiger's face.
5. Color the rest of the tiger orange.
6. Draw tall, green grass for the tiger to sleep in.

29

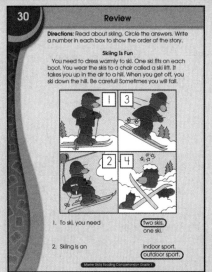

30 **Review**

Directions: Read about skiing. Circle the answers. Write a number in each box to show the order of the story.

Skiing Is Fun

You need to dress warmly to ski. One ski fits on each boot. You wear the skis to a chair called a ski lift. It takes you up in the air to a hill. When you get off, you ski down the hill. Be careful! Sometimes you will fall.

1. To ski, you need — (two skis.) / one ski.
2. Skiing is an — indoor sport. / (outdoor sport.)

30

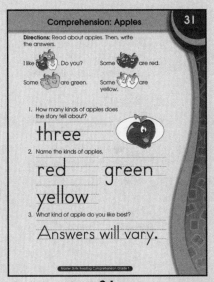

Comprehension: Apples 31

Directions: Read about apples. Then, write the answers.

I like apples. Do you? Some apples are red. Some apples are green. Some apples are yellow.

1. How many kinds of apples does the story tell about?
three

2. Name the kinds of apples.
red   green   yellow

3. What kind of apple do you like best?
Answers will vary.

31

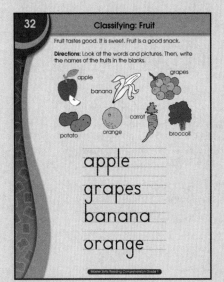

32 **Classifying: Fruit**

Fruit tastes good. It is sweet. Fruit is a good snack.

Directions: Look at the words and pictures. Then, write the names of the fruits in the blanks.

apple   banana   grapes   potato   orange   carrot   broccoli

apple
grapes
banana
orange

32

Classifying: Vegetables 33

Vegetables grow in gardens. Vegetables help keep us healthy.

Directions: Look at the pictures. Then, write the name of the vegetables in the blanks.

beans   bread   banana   lettuce   carrot   noodles   peas   broccoli

beans
lettuce
carrot
peas
broccoli

Add the name of one more vegetable.
Answers will vary.

33

34 **Comprehension: How We Eat**

Directions: Read the story. Use words from the box to answer the questions.

People eat with spoons and forks. They use a spoon to eat soup and ice cream. They use a fork to eat potatoes. They use a knife to cut their meat. They say, "Thank you. It was good!" when they finish.

fork   ice cream   knife   soup

1. What do we use to cut food?
a knife

2. What are two things you can eat with a spoon?
ice cream   soup

3. What do we use to eat meat and potatoes?
fork and knife

34

Master Skills Reading Comprehension Grade 1

Classifying: Foods 35

Directions: Read the questions under each plate. Draw three foods on each plate to answer the questions.

Drawings will vary.

1. What foods can you cut with a knife?
2. What foods should you eat with a fork?
3. What foods can you eat with a spoon?

Master Skills Reading Comprehension Grade 1

35

36 **Comprehension: Familiar Objects**

Directions: Write each word next to its picture in the puzzle.

Directions: Complete the sentences. Write the answers in the blanks.

5. I can carry things in a **bag**
6. I like to eat a red **apple**
7. I wish I could fly like a **bird**
8. I can bake a **cookie**

Master Skills Reading Comprehension Grade 1

36

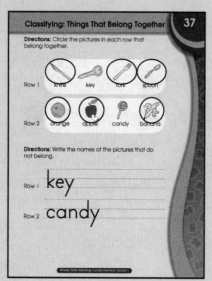

Classifying: Things That Belong Together 37

Directions: Circle the pictures in each row that belong together.

Row 1: knife, key, fork, spoon
Row 2: orange, apple, candy, banana

Directions: Write the names of the pictures that do not belong.

Row 1 **key**

Row 2 **candy**

Master Skills Reading Comprehension Grade 1

37

38 **Classifying: Why They Are Different**

Directions: Look at your answers on page 37. Write why each object does not belong.

Row 1 **You don't eat with a key.**

Row 2 **A candy is not a fruit.**

Directions: For each object, draw a group of pictures that belong with it.

candy bar — Drawings will vary.

lettuce — Drawings will vary.

Master Skills Reading Comprehension Grade 1

38

Comprehension: Write a Party Invitation 39

Directions: Read about the party. Then, complete the invitation.

The party will be at Dog's house. The party will start at 1:00 p.m. It will last two hours. Write your birthday for the date of the party.

Party Invitation

Where: **Dog's house**
Date: **Answers will vary.**
Time It Begins: **1:00 p.m.**
Time It Ends: **3:00 p.m.**

Master Skills Reading Comprehension Grade 1

39

40 **Sequencing: Pig Gets Ready**

Directions: Number the pictures of Pig getting ready for the party to show the order of the story.

3 · 1
4 · 2

What kind of party do you think Pig is going to?

Answers will vary.

Master Skills Reading Comprehension Grade 1

40

41 — Comprehension: An Animal Party

Directions: Use the picture for clues. Write words from the box to answer the questions.

bear
dog
giraffe
pig
cat
elephant
hippo
tiger

ANIMAL PARTY!

1. Which animals have bow ties?

cat   tiger

2. Which animal has a hat?

bear

3. Which animal has a striped shirt?

pig

41

42 — Classifying: Party Items

Directions: Draw a ☐ around objects that are food for the party. Draw a △ around the party guests. Draw a ○ around the objects used for fun at the party.

ice cream   candy   games   tiger
noise makers   cake   garbage can   cat
glasses   candle   bear   mice
balloons   giraffe   pig
potato chips   hippo

42

43 — Review

Directions: Read about cookies. Then, write your answers.

Cookies are made with many things. All cookies are made with flour. Some cookies have nuts in them. Some cookies do not. Some cookies have chocolate chips. Some do not. Cookbooks give directions on how to make cookies.

First, turn on the oven. Then, get out all the things that go in the cookies. Mix them together. Roll them out, and cut the cookies. Bake the cookies. Now, eat them!

1. Tell one way all cookies are the same.

All cookies are made with flour.

2. Answers may include:

nuts or chocolate chips

3. Where do you find directions for making cookies?

in cookbooks

43

44 — Comprehension: The Teddy Bear Song

Do you know the Teddy Bear Song? It is very old!

Directions: Read the Teddy Bear Song. Then, answer the questions.

Teddy bear, teddy bear, turn around.
Teddy bear, teddy bear, touch the ground.
Teddy bear, teddy bear, climb upstairs.
Teddy bear, teddy bear, say your prayers.
Teddy bear, teddy bear, turn out the light.
Teddy bear, teddy bear, say, "Good night!"

1. What is the first thing the teddy bear does?

He turns around.

2. What is the last thing the teddy bear does?

He says, "Good night!"

3. What would you name a teddy bear?

Answers will vary.

44

45 — Following Directions: Make a Teddy Bear

Directions: Color and cut out the teddy bear. Act out the song on page 44 with your teddy bear.

45

47 — Comprehension: A New Teddy Bear Song

Directions: Write words to make a new teddy bear song. Act out your new song with your teddy bear as you read it.

Answers will vary.

Teddy bear, teddy bear, turn

Teddy bear, teddy bear, touch the

Teddy bear, teddy bear, climb

Teddy bear, teddy bear, turn out

Teddy bear, teddy bear, say.

47

114

Answer Key

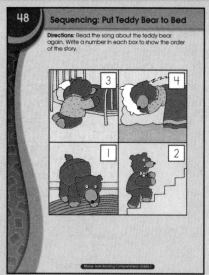

48 — Sequencing: Put Teddy Bear to Bed

Directions: Read the song about the teddy bear again. Write a number in each box to show the order of the story.

48

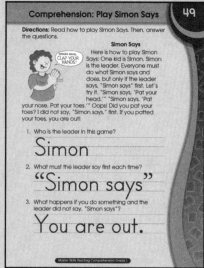

49 — Comprehension: Play Simon Says

Directions: Read how to play Simon Says. Then, answer the questions.

Simon Says

Here is how to play Simon Says: One kid is Simon. Simon is the leader. Everyone must do what Simon says and does, but only if the leader says, "Simon says" first. Let's try it. "Simon says, 'Pat your head.'" "Simon says, 'Pat your nose. Pat your toes.'" Oops! Did you pat your toes? I did not say, "Simon says." first. If you patted your toes, you are out!

1. Who is the leader in this game?

Simon

2. What must the leader say first each time?

"Simon says"

3. What happens if you do something and the leader did not say, "Simon says"?

You are out.

49

50 — Comprehension: Play Simon Says

Directions: Read each sentence. Look at the picture next to it. Circle the picture if the person is playing Simon Says correctly.

1. Simon says, "Put your hands on your hips."
2. Simon says, "Stand on one leg."
3. Simon says, "Put your hands on your head."
4. Simon says, "Ride a bike."
5. Simon says, "Jump up and down."
6. Simon says, "Pet a dog."

50

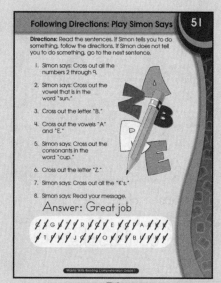

51 — Following Directions: Play Simon Says

Directions: Read the sentences. If Simon tells you to do something, follow the directions. If Simon does not tell you to do something, go to the next sentence.

1. Simon says: Cross out all the numbers 2 through 9.
2. Simon says: Cross out the vowel that is in the word "sun."
3. Cross out the letter "B."
4. Cross out the vowels "A" and "E."
5. Simon says: Cross out the consonants in the word "cup."
6. Cross out the letter "Z."
7. Simon says: Cross out all the "K's."
8. Simon says: Read your message.

Answer: Great job

51

52 — Same and Different: Look at Simon

Directions: Find four things in picture #2 that are not in picture #1. Write your answers. Use words from the box.

| hat | head | bare feet | socks |
| feather | watch | untied shoes | shirt |

1. feather
2. socks
3. watch
4. untied shoes

52

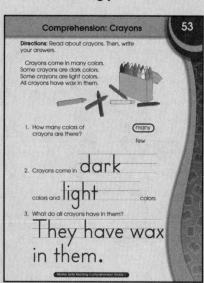

53 — Comprehension: Crayons

Directions: Read about crayons. Then, write your answers.

Crayons come in many colors. Some crayons are dark colors. Some crayons are light colors. All crayons have wax in them.

1. How many colors of crayons are there? many
2. Crayons come in dark colors and light colors.
3. What do all crayons have in them?

They have wax in them.

53

Master Skills Reading Comprehension Grade 1

Answer Key

54 — Following Directions: Hidden Picture

Directions: To find the hidden picture, color only the shapes with a number inside.

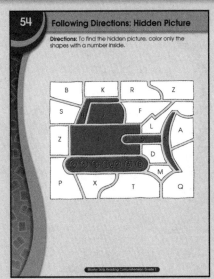

54

55 — Comprehension: Rhymes

Directions: Read about words that rhyme. Then, circle the answers.

Words that rhyme have the same end sounds. "Wing" and "sing" rhyme. "Boy" and "toy" rhyme. "Dime" and "time" rhyme. Can you think of other words that rhyme?

1. Words that rhyme have the same — (end sounds.) / end letters.

2. "Time" rhymes with — "tree." / (dime.)

Directions: Write one rhyme for each word.

wing   boy

Answers will vary.

dime   pink

55

56 — Classifying: Rhymes

Directions: Circle the pictures in each row that rhyme.

Row 1

Row 2

Row 3

Directions: Write the names of the pictures that do not rhyme.

These words do not rhyme:

Row 1	Row 2	Row 3
fan	cat	hat

56

57 — Classifying: Rhymes

Directions: Cut out the pieces. Read the words. Find two words that rhyme. Put the words together.

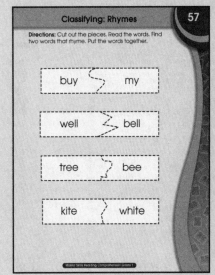

buy   my

well   bell

tree   bee

kite   white

57

59 — Review

Directions: Read about ways you move. Circle the correct answer.

You can move in many ways. You can run. When you run, one foot hits the ground at a time. You can jump. When you jump, you land on two feet. You can hop. To hop, first stand on one leg. Then, jump up and down.

1. Running and jumping are different because:

(One foot hits the ground at a time when you run. Two feet hit the ground at a time when you jump.)

Two feet hit the ground at a time when you run. One foot hits the ground at a time when you jump.

Directions: Write directions on how to hop.

2. First, stand on one leg

3. Then, jump up and down

59

60 — Comprehension: Babies

Directions: Read about babies. Then, write the answers.

Babies are small. Some babies cry a lot. They cry when they are wet. They cry when they are hungry. They smile when they are dry. They smile when they are fed.

1. Name two reasons babies cry.

hungry wet

2. Name two reasons babies smile.

dry   fed

3. Write a baby's name you like.

Answers will vary.

60

Master Skills Reading Comprehension Grade 1

61 — Comprehension: Babies

Directions: Read each sentence. Draw a picture of a baby's face in the box to show if she would cry or smile.

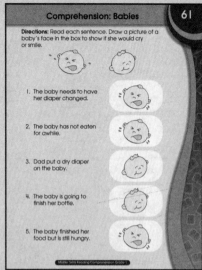

1. The baby needs to have her diaper changed.
2. The baby has not eaten for awhile.
3. Dad put a dry diaper on the baby.
4. The baby is going to finish her bottle.
5. The baby finished her food but is still hungry.

61

62 — Sequencing: Feeding Baby

Directions: Read the sentences. Write a number in each box to show the order of the story.

5 — The baby smiles.

3 — Mom makes the baby's food.

2 — The baby is put in his chair.

1 — The baby is crying.

4 — Mom feeds the baby.

62

63 — Same and Different: Compare the Twins

Directions: Read the story. Then, use the words in the box and the picture to write your answers.

Ben and Ann are twin babies. They were born at the same time. They have the same mother. Ben is a boy baby. Ann is a girl baby.

mother bow boy girl hat twins

1. Ann and Ben have the same

   mother

2. Ann and Ben are **twins**

3. Ann is a   Ben is a

   girl   **boy**

4. Ann is wearing a   Ben is wearing a

   bow   **hat**

63

64 — Comprehension: Hats

Directions: Read about hats. Then, write your answers.

There are many kinds of hats. Some baseball hats have brims. Some fancy hats have feathers. Some knit hats pull down over your ears. Some hats are made of straw. Do you like hats?

1. Name four kinds of hats.

   knit   baseball
   fancy   straw

Directions: Circle the correct answers.

2. What kind of hats pull down over your ears?

   straw hats

   (knit hats)

3. What are some hats made of?

   (straw)

   mud

64

65 — Sequencing: Choosing a Hat

Directions: Write a number in each box to show the order of the story.

65

66 — Classifying: Hats

Directions: A store has four types of hats. Draw three hats for each type listed. Write what kind of hats you think should be in the last group, and draw three of that kind.

Drawings will vary.

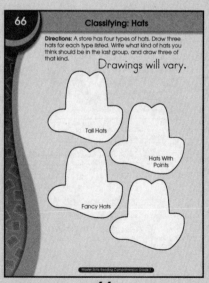

Tall Hats

Hats With Points

Fancy Hats

66

Classifying: Mr. Lincoln's Hat 67

Abraham Lincoln wore a tall hat. He liked to keep things in his hat so he would not lose them.

Directions: Cut out the pictures of things Mr. Lincoln could have kept in his hat. Glue those pictures on the hat.

67

Following Directions: Draw Hats 69

Directions: Draw a hat on each person. Read the sentences to know what kind of hat to draw.

1. The first girl is wearing a purple hat with feathers.
2. The boy next to the girl with the purple hat is wearing a red baseball hat.
3. The first boy is wearing a yellow knit hat.
4. The last boy is wearing a brown top hat.
5. The girl next to the boy with the red hat is wearing a blue straw hat.

69

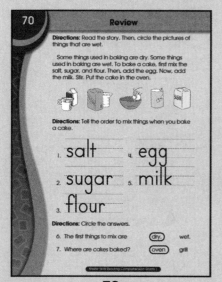

70 **Review**

Directions: Read the story. Then, circle the pictures of things that are wet.

Some things used in baking are dry. Some things used in baking are wet. To bake a cake, first mix the salt, sugar, and flour. Then, add the egg. Now, add the milk. Stir. Put the cake in the oven.

Directions: Tell the order to mix things when you bake a cake.

1. salt
2. sugar
3. flour
4. egg
5. milk

Directions: Circle the answers.

6. The first things to mix are (dry.) wet.
7. Where are cakes baked? (oven) grill

70

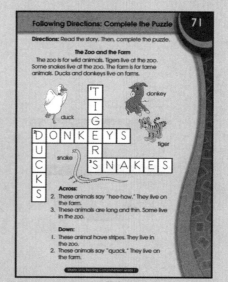

Following Directions: Complete the Puzzle 71

Directions: Read the story. Then, complete the puzzle.

The Zoo and the Farm
The zoo is for wild animals. Tigers live at the zoo. Some snakes live at the zoo. The farm is for tame animals. Ducks and donkeys live on farms.

Across:
2. These animals say "hee-haw." They live on the farm.
3. These animals are long and thin. Some live in the zoo.

Down:
1. These animal have stripes. They live in the zoo.
2. These animals say "quack." They live on the farm.

71

72 **Comprehension: Farm Sounds**

Directions: Read the story. Then, answer the questions.

You can hear many sounds on the farm. Roosters crow in the morning. The cows moo, and donkeys say, "hee-haw." You might even hear the tractor motor humming.

1. What sound does the cow make?

moo

2. What animal crows in the morning?

rooster

3. What animal says "hee-haw"?

donkey

Directions: Circle the farm words in the puzzle. Look up and down and sideways.

donkey   rooster
moo   tractor

72

Same and Different: Compare the Barnyards 73

Directions: Look at the pictures of the barnyards. Color the five things in picture #1 that are different from picture #2.

73

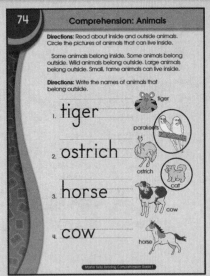

74 · Comprehension: Animals

Directions: Read about inside and outside animals. Circle the pictures of animals that can live inside.

Some animals belong inside. Some animals belong outside. Wild animals belong outside. Large animals belong outside. Small, tame animals can live inside.

Directions: Write the names of animals that belong outside.

1. tiger
2. ostrich
3. horse
4. cow

74

75 · Comprehension: Days

Directions: Read about the days of the week. Then, answer the questions.

Do you know the names of the seven days of the week? Here they are: Sunday, Monday, Tuesday, Wednesday, Thursday, Friday, and Saturday.

1. What day comes after Thursday?
Friday

2. What day comes before Tuesday?
Monday

3. How many days are in each week?
seven

75

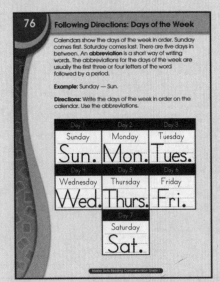

76 · Following Directions: Days of the Week

Calendars show the days of the week in order. Sunday comes first. Saturday comes last. There are five days in between. An **abbreviation** is a short way of writing words. The abbreviations for the days of the week are usually the first three or four letters of the word followed by a period.

Example: Sunday — Sun.

Directions: Write the days of the week in order on the calendar. Use the abbreviations.

Day 1	Day 2	Day 3
Sunday	Monday	Tuesday
Sun.	Mon.	Tues.
Day 4	Day 5	Day 6
Wednesday	Thursday	Friday
Wed.	Thurs.	Fri.
	Day 7	
	Saturday	
	Sat.	

76

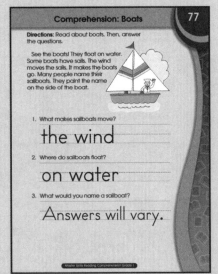

77 · Comprehension: Boats

Directions: Read about boats. Then, answer the questions.

See the boats! They float on water. Some boats have sails. The wind moves the sails. It makes the boats go. Many people name their sailboats. They paint the name on the side of the boat.

1. What makes sailboats move?
the wind

2. Where do sailboats float?
on water

3. What would you name a sailboat?
Answers will vary.

77

78 · Same and Different: Color the Boats

Directions: Find the three boats that are alike. Color them all the same. One boat is different. Color it differently.

78

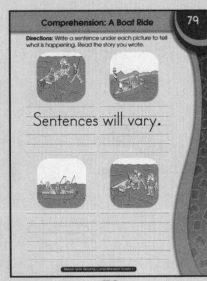

79 · Comprehension: A Boat Ride

Directions: Write a sentence under each picture to tell what is happening. Read the story you wrote.

Sentences will vary.

79

80 — Comprehension: Travel

Directions: Read the story. Then, answer the questions.

Let's Take a Trip!
Pack your bag. Shall we go by car, plane, or train? Let's go to the sea. When we get there, let's go on a sailboat.

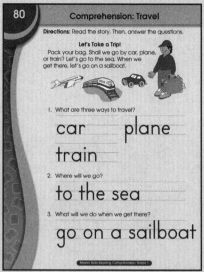

1. What are three ways to travel?

car   plane
train

2. Where will we go?

to the sea

3. What will we do when we get there?

go on a sailboat

Master Skills Reading Comprehension Grade 1

80

81 — Following Directions: Draw a Path

Directions: Read about how to get to the beach. Use a crayon to draw the path to the beach.

Let's Go to the Beach
On the way to the beach, you will stop for food, then gas. Next, you cross a bridge. Finally, you will be at the beach!

Master Skills Reading Comprehension Grade 1

81

82 — Review

Directions: Read the story. Then, write the answers.

Fun With Balls
Some balls are soft. A beach ball is soft. Some balls are hard. We play baseball with a hard ball. Basketballs bounce. Can you throw a basketball through a hoop? First, bounce it three times. Then, hold the basketball high. Now, throw it toward the hoop. Did you make a basket?

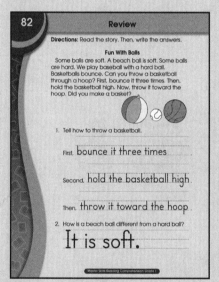

1. Tell how to throw a basketball.

First. bounce it three times.

Second. hold the basketball high.

Then. throw it toward the hoop.

2. How is a beach ball different from a hard ball?

It is soft.

Master Skills Reading Comprehension Grade 1

82

83 — Comprehension: Clocks

Directions: Read about clocks. Then, answer the questions.

Ticking Clocks
Many clocks make two sounds. The sounds are tick and tock. Big clocks often make loud tick-tocks. Little clocks often make quiet tick-tocks. Sometimes people put little clocks in a box with a new puppy. The puppy likes the sound. The tick-tock makes the puppy feel safe.

1. What two sounds do many clocks make?

tick   and   tock

2. What kind of tick-tocks do big clocks make?

loud tick tocks

3. What kind of clock makes a new puppy feel safe?

a little clock

Master Skills Reading Comprehension Grade 1

83

84 — Sequencing: Help the Puppy Feel Safe

Directions: Read the story about clocks again. Then, write a number in each box to show the order of the story.

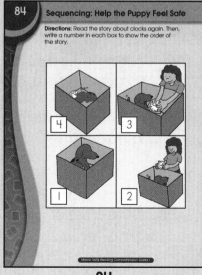

4   3
1   2

Master Skills Reading Comprehension Grade 1

84

85 — Same and Different: These Don't Belong

Directions: Circle the pictures in each row that go together.

Row 1   cookies   cake   beans   ice cream

Row 2   apple   banana   orange   cookies

Directions: Write the names of the things that do not belong.

Row 1   beans

Row 2   cookies

Master Skills Reading Comprehension Grade 1

85

86

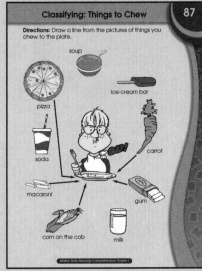

87

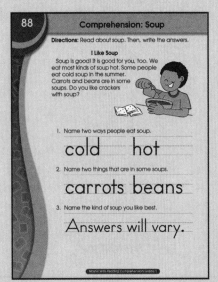

88

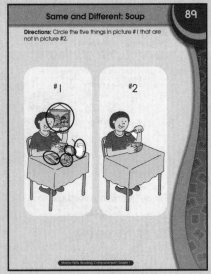

89

90

91

92

Following Directions: Three Bears Puzzle

Directions: Read the story about the three bears again. Then, complete the puzzle.

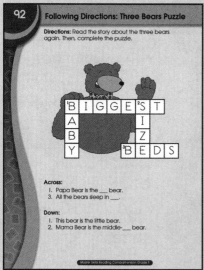

¹BIGGE'S²T
A   I
B   Z
Y   ³BEDS

Across:
1. Papa Bear is the ___ bear.
3. All the bears sleep in ___.

Down:
1. This bear is the little bear.
2. Mama Bear is the middle-___ bear.

Master Skills Reading Comprehension Grade 1

92

93

Review

Directions: Read how to make no-cook candy. Then, answer the questions.

Some candy needs to be cooked on a stove. You do not need to cook this kind of candy. It is easy to make. You will need a large bowl for mixing. You will need five things to make this candy.

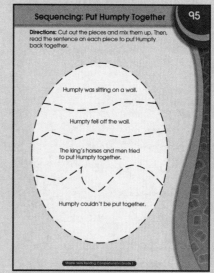

No-Cook Candy
½ cup peanut butter
4 cups powdered sugar
1 cup cocoa
pinch of salt
4 tablespoons milk
Mix everything in the bowl. Roll it into small balls. (A pinch of salt is just a tiny bit.)

1. What is third on the list of things needed?

I cup cocoa

2. What is different about no-cook candy?

You don't have to cook it.

Directions: Write what to do to make no-cook candy.

3. First, mix everything in a bowl. Then,

Roll it into small balls.

Master Skills Reading Comprehension Grade 1

93

94

Comprehension: "Humpty Dumpty"

Directions: Read the poem. Draw a picture of Humpty Dumpty after he fell off the wall.

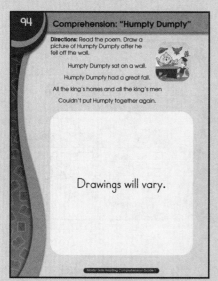

Humpty Dumpty sat on a wall.

Humpty Dumpty had a great fall.

All the king's horses and all the king's men

Couldn't put Humpty together again.

Drawings will vary.

Master Skills Reading Comprehension Grade 1

94

95

Sequencing: Put Humpty Together

Directions: Cut out the pieces and mix them up. Then, read the sentence on each piece to put Humpty back together.

Humpty was sitting on a wall.

Humpty fell off the wall.

The king's horses and men tried to put Humpty together.

1

Humpty couldn't be put together.

Master Skills Reading Comprehension Grade 1

95

97

Comprehension: "Hey Diddle Diddle"

Directions: Read "Hey Diddle Diddle." Then, answer the questions.

Hey diddle diddle.

The cat and the fiddle.

The cow jumped over the moon.

The little dog laughed

To see such sport,

And the dish ran away with the spoon!

1. Who jumped over the moon?

the cow

2. Who laughed?

the little dog

3. Who ran away?

dish and spoon

Master Skills Reading Comprehension Grade 1

97

98

Comprehension: "Hey Diddle Diddle"

Directions: Read "Hey Diddle Diddle" again. Then, answer the questions.

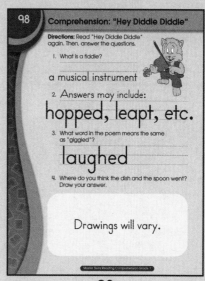

1. What is a fiddle?

a musical instrument

2. Answers may include:

hopped, leapt, etc.

3. What word in the poem means the same as "giggled"?

laughed

4. Where do you think the dish and the spoon went? Draw your answer.

Drawings will vary.

Master Skills Reading Comprehension Grade 1

98

Answer Key

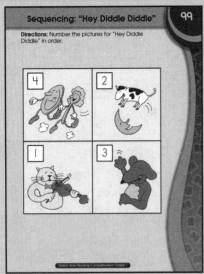

Sequencing: "Hey Diddle Diddle" 99

Directions: Number the pictures for "Hey Diddle Diddle" in order.

Master Skills Reading Comprehension Grade 1

99

---

100 **Comprehension: "Bluebird"**

Directions: Read the bluebird poem. Look at the picture. Write what the bluebird sees. Use words from the box.

Bluebird, bluebird.
Up in the tree.
How many blue things
Do you see?

book	flowers
girl	grass
hat	sky
shoes	tree

Here are the blue things the bluebird sees:

1. book   4. hat
2. sky   5. flowers
3. shoes

Master Skills Reading Comprehension Grade 1

100

Comprehension: "New Bird" 101

Directions: Fill in the blanks to create a poem about a different colored bird. Then, draw a picture in the box to go with your poem. **Answers will vary.**

_____ bird. _____ bird.

Up in the _____

How many _____ things

Do you see?

Drawings will vary.

Directions: Fill in the blanks. **Answers will vary.**

How many _____ things did the bird

see in your picture?

Master Skills Reading Comprehension Grade 1

101

---

102 **Sequencing: Make an Ice-Cream Cone**

Directions: Number the boxes in order to show how to make an ice-cream cone.

Master Skills Reading Comprehension Grade 1

102

Comprehension: Eating Ice Cream 103

Directions: Read the story. Write two things Sam could have done so he could have enjoyed eating his ice-cream cone.

It was a hot day. Sam went to the store and got an ice-cream cone. He ate it at a table in the sun. Sam watched some friends play ball. When he went to eat his ice-cream, it had melted and fallen on the sidewalk.

1. **Answers will vary.**

2. _____

Master Skills Reading Comprehension Grade 1

103

---

104 **Sequencing: Eating a Cone**

What if a person never ate an ice-cream cone? Could you tell them how to eat it? Think about what you do when you eat an ice-cream cone.

Directions: Write directions to teach someone how to eat an ice-cream cone.

How to Eat an Ice-Cream Cone

1. **Answers will vary.**

2. _____

3. _____

4. _____

Master Skills Reading Comprehension Grade 1

104

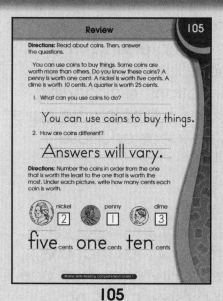

105

The goal of reading is to understand what is read. In addition to saying the words, your child needs to comprehend what the words are telling him or her. Learning skills such as classifying, comprehension, following directions, recognizing similarities and differences, and sequencing will help your child become a better reader. You can use the ideas on these pages to help your child master these skills.

Classifying

Classifying involves putting objects, words, or ideas that are alike into categories. Items can be classified in more than one way. For example, hats could be sorted by size, color, or season worn. If your child creates a category you had not considered, praise him or her for thinking creatively.

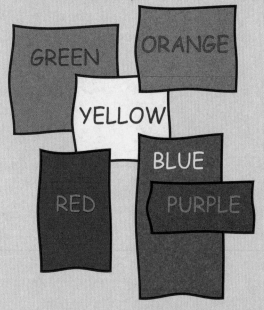

Your child could sort the clothing in his or her closet. He or she could sort it according to the season each item is worn, by color, type of clothing, or even likes and dislikes. You can have your child help you sort laundry by colors.

At the grocery store, talk about the layout of the store and how items are arranged in the store. For example, fruits are together, vegetables are together, cooking supplies are together, soups are together, etc. Talk about why items would be arranged in groups like that. What would happen if they were not arranged in groups?

Have your child help you find what you need by having him or her decide what section of the store it would be in. After finding the item, talk about alternate places the item could be found.

When planning a family vacation, collect travel brochures on possible destinations and sites to see. Have your child classify the brochures according to location, activity, or places you may or may not want to visit. Use these groupings to plan your trip.

Comprehension

Comprehension involves understanding what is seen, heard, or read. To help your child with this skill, talk about a book, picture, movie, or television program. Ask your child if he or she likes it and the reasons why or why not. By listening to what he or she says, you can tell whether the book, etc., was understood. If your child does not fully understand part of it, discuss that section further. Reread the book or watch the program again, if possible.

Your child can make a poster for a book or movie. Have him or her include the important events, most exciting parts, favorite part, and reasons why someone else should view or read it.

Watch the news with your child and discuss the job of a news reporter. After your child understands what reporters do, create your own newscast. You can be the reporter, and your child can pretend to be a character from a book or movie. Make up the questions together, based on a book read or movie watched. Use the questions for an "interview." If you have a video camera, record your interview, and play it back for your child to watch.

Teaching Suggestions

After reading a book, have your child create a book cover for it. The picture should tell about the book and include a brief summary on the back. If the book belongs to your child, he or she could use the cover on the book.

Find a cartoon without words or cut a cartoon from the newspaper and cut off the words. Have your child look at the pictures and create words to go along with the pictures. If your child has difficulty writing, you can write what he or she says.

Following Directions

Cooking is one of many daily activities that involves following directions. Whether it is heating a can of soup, cooking a frozen dinner, or making a box of pudding, all involve following directions. Read the package directions with your child and have him or her help you.

When you have a shelving unit, table, toy, etc., to assemble, allow your child to help. Point to each step in the directions. Read each step out loud together. Then, follow the steps in order.

Like following package directions or a recipe, assembling an item enables your child to see that following directions is a skill used in everyday situations.

Building a model and making craft projects are other ways for your child to learn to follow directions. Rather than a store-bought model, you could make your own by precutting wood pieces to make a birdhouse or other small item. Write step-by-step directions for your child. Then, use the directions with your child to actually make it.

Each day, make a list of the jobs your child needs to complete. Then, your child can follow the list to complete the jobs. If your child has difficulty reading, you can draw small pictures to represent each job. You know your child is able to follow directions when tasks are completed correctly.

Same and Different

This skill involves being able to tell how things are alike and not alike. This can easily be incorporated into daily activities. For instance, when driving in a car, have your child compare objects seen, such as cars and trucks, telling how they are the same and how they are different.

At home or in the grocery store, compare foods such as green apples and pears, or broccoli and beans asking your child for ideas about how they are the same and different. Your child can also compare the taste and texture of the foods.

When shopping for clothes, ask your child how two shirts, pairs of pants, or shoes look the same and different. Then, if your child tries them on, he or she can compare how they fit.

Outside, your child can compare types of flowers or trees. Besides the physical characteristics like color, size, and smell, also compare the needs of plants, such as water, sun, and soil.

Your child can compare objects verbally or create a chart to record the similarities and differences. He or she can make lists that show objects that are the same and different.

Sequencing

Sequencing involves putting things in order. This can include steps to complete a task, sizes of object, or the time events occur during the day. To help your child with sequencing, get a comic strip that has three or four sections and read it with your child. Cut the sections apart and then have your child put it back together. If this is too difficult for your child, use a strip with only two sections at first.

In the morning, tell your child three steps involved in making his or her bed. Have your child tell you the order of the steps and then actually make the bed. At the end of the day, your child can put away the toys in a specific order, such as from smallest to largest or lightest to heaviest.

Have your child keep a journal. This not only helps with sequencing, but it is a good way to record what is happening in his or her life for the future. Each night in the journal, have your child write or draw four things that he or she did during the day.